A Guide for Using

Shiloh

in the Classroom

Based on the novel written by
Phyllis Reynolds Naylor

This guide written by
Gabriel Arquilevich, M.F.A.

Teacher Created Materials, Inc.
6421 Industry Way
Westminster, CA 92683
www.teachercreated.com
©*1996 Teacher Created Materials, Inc.*
Reprinted, 2001
Made in U.S.A.
ISBN 1-55734-566-X

Illustrated by
Ken Tunell

Edited by
Cathy Gilbert, M.A.

Cover Art by
Agi Palinay

Table of Contents

Introduction

A good book is unforgettable. Like a friend, it can touch our lives, inspiring us to honesty and greatness. We turn to our favorite literature for companionship, guidance, and recreation.

In *Literature Units*, great care has been taken to select quality books, books that are sure to become good friends!

This unit features the following ideas:

- Sample Lesson Plans
- Pre-reading Activities
- Biographical Sketch
- Book Summary
- Vocabulary Lists and Suggested Vocabulary Ideas
- Chapters grouped for study, with each section including:

  —a quiz

  —a hands-on project

  —a cooperative learning activity

  —cross-curriculum connections

  —extension into the reader's life

- Post-reading Activities
- Book Report Ideas
- Research Activities
- Culminating Activities
- Three Different Options for Unit Tests
- Bibliography of Related Readings
- Answer Key

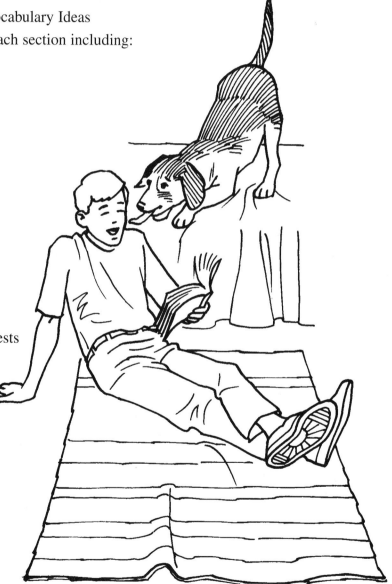

We are confident this unit will be a valuable addition to your planning, and we hope that as you use our ideas, your students will fall in love with reading.

Sample Lesson Plan

Each of the lessons suggested below can take from one to several days to complete.

Lesson 1

- Introduce some or all of the pre-reading activities.
- Read "About the Author" with your students. (page 6)
- Read the book summary with your students. (page 7)
- Introduce Section 1 vocabulary list. (page 8)
- Discuss "Active Reading" with your students. (page 10)

Lesson 2

- Read chapters 1–3. As you read, place the vocabulary words in the context of the story and discuss their meanings.
- Do a vocabulary activity. (page 9)
- Make a montage. (page 12)
- Do animal rights project. (page 13)
- Complete "West Virginia Facts." (page 14)
- Do map skills. (page 15)
- Begin Reading Response Journals. (page 16)
- Administer the Section 1 Quiz. (page 11)
- Introduce Section 2 vocabulary list. (page 8)

Lesson 3

- Read chapters 4–7. Place vocabulary words in context and discuss meanings.
- Do a vocabulary activity. (page 9)
- Build a pen. (page 18)
- Do theater games. (page 19)
- Complete recycling project. (page 20)
- Do a word portrait of an animal. (page 21)
- Administer the Section 2 quiz. (page 17)
- Introduce Section 3 vocabulary list. (page 8)

Lesson 4

- Read chapters 8–11. Place vocabulary words in context and discuss meanings.
- Do a vocabulary activity. (page 9)

- Cook some "Preston" food. (page 23)
- Conduct a mock trial. (page 24)
- Do point-of-view practice. (page 25)
- Complete research on Beagles. (page 26)
- Discuss rural and urban life. (page 27)
- Discuss "What Would You Do?" (page 28)
- Administer the Section 3 quiz. (page 22)
- Introduce Section 4 vocabulary list. (page 8)

Lesson 5

- Read chapters 12–15. Place vocabulary words in context and discuss meanings.
- Do a vocabulary activity. (page 9)
- Conduct storytelling. (page 30)
- Complete "A Closer Look." (page 31)
- Discuss and interpret dialect. (page 32)
- Discuss and interpret personal ethics and lies. (page 33)
- Answer reflection questions. (page 34)
- Administer the Section 4 quiz. (page 29)

Lesson 6

- Discuss any questions your students have about the story. (page 35)
- Complete descriptive writing activity. (page 36)
- Assign book report and research activity. (pages 37 and 38)
- Begin culminating activity. (page 39)

Lesson 7

- Administer Unit Tests: 1, 2, and/or 3. (pages 42, 43, and 44)
- Discuss the test answers and possibilities.
- Discuss the students' enjoyment of the book.
- Provide a list of related readings for your students. (page 45)
- Provide students with a copy of Phyllis Reynolds Naylor's letter. (page 46)

Before the Book

Before you begin reading *Shiloh*, do some pre-reading activities to stimulate interest and enhance comprehension. The following activities might work well for your class. Feel free to extend these activities!

1. Predict what the story might be about by studying the cover illustration.
2. Discuss other books by Phyllis Reynolds Naylor that the students may have heard about or read.
3. Discuss the Newbery Medal. What is it? Who awards it? Have students list other books which have won this prestigious award.

   Since 1922, the American Library Association has awarded the Newbery Medal to the most distinguished contribution to children's literature published the preceding year. The Newbery Medal was named for John Newbery, the first English publisher of books for children. One or more books are also named as "honor" books.

4. Have students find the copyright date and publisher of *Shiloh*.
5. *Shiloh* is a story about a boy and a dog. Have students brainstorm a list of other dog and animal stories. What do they have in common? How do they differ?
6. Ask students to think about the following questions and decide how they would respond to each of them.

Are you interested in:

— stories about animals?

— stories dealing with young people having experiences that make them become more mature?

— stories told from the point of view of someone your own age?

— stories about someone your own age taking a stand for something he or she believes in?

— stories with a "bad guy"?

   Is it ever okay to break the law?

   Have you ever really wanted something but not had the money to afford it?

   Have you ever had to lie to your parents?

7. Working in groups, have students brainstorm and describe the qualities of a courageous, honest person. How does such a person gain his or her integrity? Is integrity physical, emotional, or spiritual?

About the Author

Phyllis Reynolds Naylor was born on January 4, 1933, in Anderson, Indiana. Although she grew up during the Great Depression, her life was enriched by storytelling, reading, and writing. When she was not allowed to use new paper for writing, she would, in her own words, "rush home from school to see if the wastebasket held any discarded paper." There she would write down whatever plot had been forming in her head.

Naylor's first published story appeared in a church magazine when she was 16. She was even able to pay her tuition through college by writing stories. Later she began writing a column for teenagers, a column that continued for 25 years. After earning a bachelor's degree in psychology from American University, Mrs. Naylor devoted herself to raising a family and writing. In 1965 she published her first complete book, *The Galloping Goat and Other Stories.* She has since published over 80 works, including books for children and adults. Her work has earned her numerous awards and honors, including The South Carolina Young Adult Book Award, 1985–86, for *A String of Chances*; the Edgar Allan Poe Award for *Night Cry;* and the coveted Newbery Medal for *Shiloh.*

Like *Shiloh,* many of Mrs. Naylor's novels for young adults tackle difficult and sensitive issues. In *A String of Chances*, a preacher's daughter questions her faith when her cousin's baby dies. In *The Solomon System,* two brothers face the complexity and sorrow of their parents' divorce.

Several books written by Mrs. Naylor are inspired by real-life situations. *Shiloh* is no exception. According to Mrs. Naylor, "The first part of the story, the way Marty Preston found Shiloh along the river, is true. That's the way I came across a skinny, trembling dog who became Shiloh in my story. It followed my husband and me back to the home of friends in the little community of Shiloh, West Virginia, just up the hill from Friendly."

Today, Naylor lives in Bethesda, Maryland with her husband, a speech pathologist. The Naylor's have two children, Jeffrey Alan and Michael Scott, now grown. She has said she is happy when spending some time each day writing—often as much as six hours. Depending on how much research is needed and how well formed her ideas about characters, she will take from three months to a year on a children's book and perhaps as much as a year or two on a novel for adults. She says "the best part about writing is the moment a character comes alive on paper . . . ." That is what she likes the best.

(Quotations and information from *Major Authors and Illustrators*, edited by Laurie Collier and Joyce Nakuma. Gale Research, Detroit: 1933, and a letter from the author.)

6

Shiloh

by Phyllis Reynolds Naylor

(Dell, 1991)

(Available in Canada from Doubleday Dell Seal; in U.K., Bantam Doubleday Dell; in AUS, Transworld Pub.)

Like many of Phyllis Reynolds Naylor's novels, *Shiloh*, set in the rural town of Friendly, West Virginia, grapples with sensitive issues. In this story, Marty Preston, a boy of eleven, must deal with deep ethical questions. Right and wrong, good and evil, and truth and lies all become muddled when Marty finds Shiloh, a stray beagle. Marty is convinced that the dog is being abused by its owner, the mean-spirited Judd Travers. As Marty's love for Shiloh grows, he is determined to keep the dog at all costs. Because his family is poor and without the money to feed another mouth, his parents do not want any pets. Desperate, Marty builds Shiloh a shelter on the hill near his home, hiding him from both Judd and his own family. He spends his days collecting scraps of food for Shiloh and then sneaking off to play with his beloved beagle.

Although happy about Shiloh, Marty is deeply torn about lying to his family and friends. The lies escalate, leaving Marty confused: he must choose between lying or giving Shiloh back to Judd Travers. But Marty is also angry. While most of the people in Friendly know that Judd Travers mistreats his animals, no one speaks out. This conflict is most acute during his conversations with his father when Marty learns that the "grown up" world is not always fair.

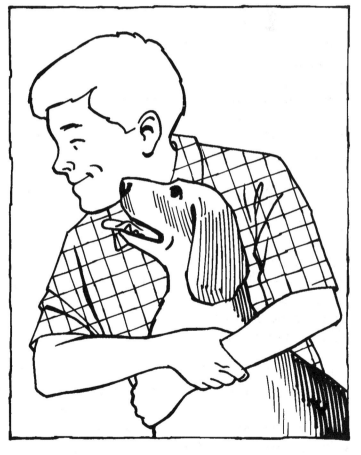

Marty's secret cannot last. When Marty's mom catches him and Shiloh, she agrees to keep quiet for one night, implicating herself in the chain of lies. That night, Shiloh is badly wounded by a neighbor's German shepherd. Marty's father takes Shiloh to the town doctor, who stitches the dog's wounds and keeps him overnight.

Soon after, Shiloh returns to the Preston's home. Although his parents decide to return Shiloh, Marty refuses. When he marches to Judd's house early the next morning, he catches Judd illegally shooting a deer out of season. In exchange for Marty's silence and twenty hours of hard labor, Judd agrees to give Shiloh to Marty. Judd tries to renege on his side of the bargain, but Marty's honesty and grit somehow touch him. In the end, they learn to get along, and Shiloh belongs to Marty.

Vocabulary Lists

This page contains vocabulary lists which correspond to each sectional grouping of chapters. Vocabulary activity ideas can be found on page 9 of this book.

Although *Shiloh* does not use elevated language, it is rich with idiomatic words and phrases. Some of these will appear in our lists. Let your students know that some of the vernacular will not appear in the dictionary. On page 32, we will further explore the use of dialect.

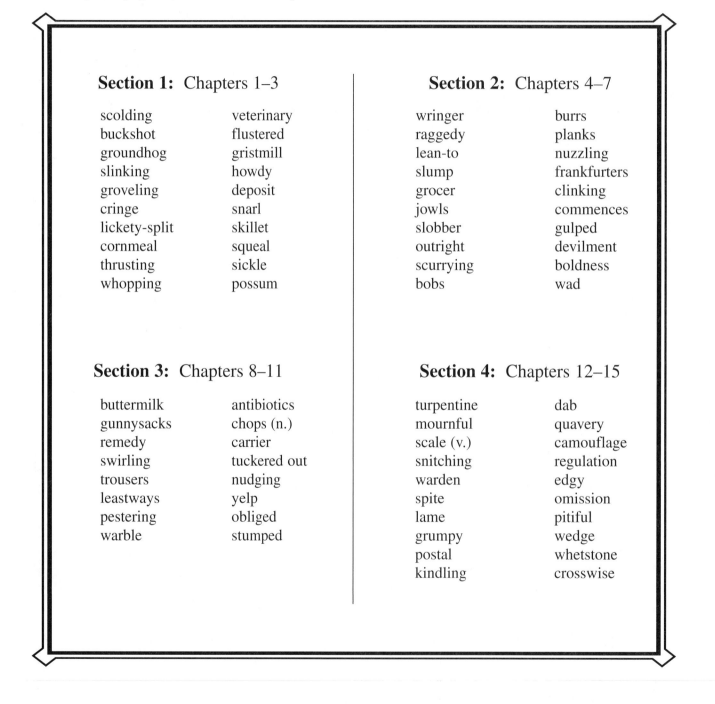

Section 1: Chapters 1–3

scolding	veterinary
buckshot	flustered
groundhog	gristmill
slinking	howdy
groveling	deposit
cringe	snarl
lickety-split	skillet
cornmeal	squeal
thrusting	sickle
whopping	possum

Section 2: Chapters 4–7

wringer	burrs
raggedy	planks
lean-to	nuzzling
slump	frankfurters
grocer	clinking
jowls	commences
slobber	gulped
outright	devilment
scurrying	boldness
bobs	wad

Section 3: Chapters 8–11

buttermilk	antibiotics
gunnysacks	chops (n.)
remedy	carrier
swirling	tuckered out
trousers	nudging
leastways	yelp
pestering	obliged
warble	stumped

Section 4: Chapters 12–15

turpentine	dab
mournful	quavery
scale (v.)	camouflage
snitching	regulation
warden	edgy
spite	omission
lame	pitiful
grumpy	wedge
postal	whetstone
kindling	crosswise

Vocabulary Activity Ideas

You can help your students learn and retain the vocabulary in *Shiloh* by providing them with interesting vocabulary activities. Here are a few ideas:

■ People of all ages like to make and solve puzzles. Ask your students to make their own **Crossword Puzzles** or **Word Search Puzzles** using the vocabulary words from the story.

■ Challenge your students to a **Vocabulary Bee**. This is similar to a spelling bee, but in addition to spelling each word correctly, the participants must correctly define the words as well.

■ Play **Vocabulary Concentration**. The goal of this game is to match vocabulary words with their definitions. Divide the class into groups of 2–5 students. Have students make two sets of cards the same size and color. On one set have them write the vocabulary words. On the second set have them write the definitions. All cards are mixed together and placed face down on a table. A player picks two cards. If the pair matches the word with its definition, the player keeps the cards and takes another turn. If the cards don't match, they are returned to their places face down on the table, and another player takes a turn. Players must concentrate to remember locations of words and their definitions. The game continues until all matches have been made. This is an ideal activity for free exploration time.

■ Have students practice their writing skills by creating sentences and paragraphs in which multiple vocabulary words are used correctly. Ask them to share their **Compact Vocabulary** sentences and paragraphs with the class.

■ Play **Hangman**, using the definition as a clue. This is a good activity to play in partners.

■ Challenge your students to use a specific vocabulary word from the story at least **10 Times in One Day**. They must keep a record of when, how, and why the word was used.

■ Have students work together to create an **Illustrated Dictionary** of the vocabulary words.

■ Play **20 Clues** with the class. One student selects a vocabulary word and gives clues about it, one by one, until someone guesses the word.

■ Play **Vocabulary Charades**. In this game, vocabulary words are acted out!

You probably have many more ideas to add to this list. Try them. See if experiencing vocabulary on a personal level increases your students' vocabulary interest and retention!

Active Reading: A Note to Teachers

Most of us—students and teachers alike—never really wonder what it means to read. Although we have spent our lives reading for school and for pleasure, we rarely think of reading as an active, dynamic experience. Have you ever, for example, thought about your own reading style? Do you quickly devour a book? Do you read slowly and allow time for reflection? Do you read a book more than once? What do you focus most of your attention on: plot? character? style? How a student reads is critical in determining what he or she receives from literature.

First of all, students should know the difference between **active** and **passive** reading. Passive reading is a little like watching television; the reader moves through the story or poem superficially. Perhaps he or she is entertained, but the depth of understanding is minimal. An active reader, on the other hand, is engaged with the material, meeting the author halfway. The active reader asks questions, looking deeply and making discoveries.

But what are the specifics of active reading? What should a reader look for? Here are some suggestions you and your students might find helpful.

- **Plot:** What happens in the book? How is the story structured?

- **Setting:** Where does the story take place? How does the setting affect the characters?

- **Character development:** How does the main character(s) change? What causes these changes to occur?

- **Point of View:** Who is telling the story? How would the story be different if it were told from another point of view?

- **Language and Tone:** How would you describe the author's writing style? Is the language formal or informal? Are the sentences long or short? Can you find a rhythm in the writing? What about the paragraphs? Are they well supported? What is the tone of the language? Is it humorous, serious, or matter of fact?

- **Meaning:** Is there a moral to the story? What has the main character(s) learned from his or her experiences? What have you learned from the book?

Before beginning *Shiloh*, discuss active reading with your students. Cover all the areas mentioned above. It is important to have them share their own reading styles and their feelings about reading.

If your students are not used to active reading, it may be demanding at first. Ultimately, though, approaching literature this way will make it more meaningful and more pleasurable.

10

Quiz Time!

1. On the back of this paper, write a one-paragraph summary of the major events in each chapter of section 1. Then complete the rest of the questions.

2. Briefly describe how Marty and Shiloh first meet. How does Shiloh behave?

   _____

   _____

3. List the three Preston children and their ages.

   _____

   _____

4. What does Mr. Preston do for work? What does Marty want to be?

   _____

   _____

5. What town and state does the story take place in? What season is it?

   _____

   _____

6. Marty gives four reasons why he doesn't like Judd Travers. List at least two of these reasons. Do you think the reasons are valid?

   _____

   _____

7. Where does Marty sleep? Why? Does he complain about it?

   _____

   _____

8. How does Judd treat Shiloh after Marty returns him? How does Marty respond?

   _____

   _____

9. What magazines does Judd subscribe to? What does this tell you about him?

   _____

   _____

10. List the ways that Marty tries to raise money.

   _____

   _____

Montage

As you read about Marty's family, you will probably make comparisons with your own family. Are you the oldest? Do you have only sisters? Maybe your family is the opposite, and you are the only girl. Or perhaps you are an only child. These differences in family structure play a part in making us who we are.

How about Marty's hometown? Are there any similarities between Marty's rural setting and your own? Can you imagine living in a place where there are no street lights? Do you have wilderness nearby where you can run and play?

Keeping Marty's living situation in mind, make a montage of your family and community. A montage is a picture made up of many separate pictures. This montage should tell the viewer about your family and/or your community. Besides pictures, you can also use drawings, maps, newspaper clippings, and photos.

Here are some other ideas for your montage:

• Look in the telephone book. Find out whether anyone has the same last name as yours. Copy that part of the page for your montage.

• Include a story of how your community got its name.

• Interview a family member about some interesting incident that happened to him or her in the community or in the history of the family. Include it as a story.

• Add photos of people, places, and things in your community.

Visit at least one of the following places in your community. Find out what people do there. Explain why the place is important to your family. Take pictures!

• town hall
• firehouse
• police station
• recycling center
• place of worship

• library
• hospital
• park or recreation center
• water department
• day care center

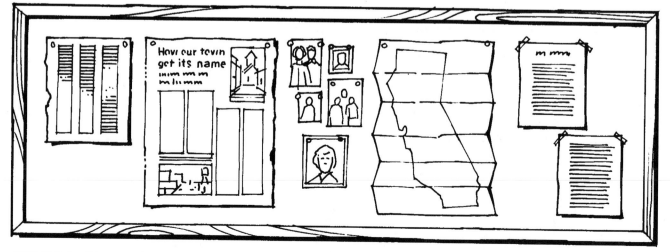

Animal Rights Research Project

"'How do you go about reporting someone who don't take care of his dog right?'"

—*Marty*

"'Law never told me before what I could do with my dogs, won't be telling me now . . . .'"

—*Judd*

"I've been thinking about it. Do I really suppose they'd send an investigator all the way out from Middlebourne to see about a man said to kick his dogs?"

—*Marty*

Imagine that you and your classmates are in the same situation as Marty: you know someone is abusing an animal. Certainly, you would share Marty's concerns and questions. What do you do? Who do you contact? What rights do animals have? What do you need to do to convince the authorities?

Your group can answer all these questions with some basic research. Begin by calling your local animal shelter or humane society and asking for the **penal codes**, or laws, regarding animals. You will be surprised to find pages of rules and standards for the care of animals. Take, for instance, this brief excerpt from California State Penal Code 597.1:

"Every owner . . . of any animal who permits the animal to be . . . without proper care and attention is guilty of a misdemeanor. Any peace officer, humane society officer, or animal control officer shall take possession of the stray or abandoned animal . . . ."

Would this information be useful to Marty?

You can also interview a humane society officer. Here are just a few questions you may want to ask.

What are some real-life accounts of animal abuse?

How many cases of animal abuse do you get in a year?

What happens to people who mistreat their animals?

What happens to animals that cannot be returned to their owners?

Are the rules as strict in rural areas as they are in urban areas?

Are mistreated animals dangerous to handle?

Are pets mistreated more often than farm animals?

Are animals in carnivals and zoos frequently mistreated ?

◆ Is it common for abuse to occur in obedience training for pets or in training of hunting dogs?

When you complete your interview and research project, present your findings to the class. Be sure to use specifics, such as quotes from interviews and penal codes, for support. End your report by declaring what you would do if you knew someone was abusing an animal.

West Virginia Facts

Directions: Use appropriate reference books to locate the following information about the state of West Virginia.

Population: _____ (ranks_____in population)

Area: _____ square miles (ranks_____in size)

Capital: _____ How many people live in the capital city? _____

State Nickname:_____ State Flower: _____

State Motto:_____

Highest Point in West Virginia: _____

Lowest Point in West Virginia:_____

Time Zone:_____ Major Industry: _____

Three largest cities and their populations:

1. _____
2. _____
3. _____

Map Skills

Now that you know some of the basic facts about West Virginia, take a more detailed look at the geography of the state. Using the map on page 15 as a reference, answer the following map skills questions. Mark the answers on the map or write the answers on the back of this paper. When you finish, go over the answers with other students in your class.

- Find the town of Friendly on the map.
- Locate the towns of Middlebourne and Shiloh.
- What major river is near Friendly?
- What state does Friendly border?
- What important city is 80 miles (128 km) southwest of Friendly?
- The eastern part of the state contains what large mountain range?

1. About how many miles and kilometers are between Friendly and Charleston?
2. Which state lies directly east of Morgantown?
3. Which state lies directly southwest of Charleston?
4. West Virginia is between which latitudes? (approximately)
5. West Virginia is between which longitudes? (approximately)
6. Give the approximate latitude and longitude of Friendly.
7. Does Highway 77 cross West Virginia north to south or east to west? About how many miles of West Virginia does the highway cover?
8. Name three lakes in West Virginia.
9. Which state lies directly south of Bluestone Lake?
10. In which hemisphere is West Virginia? (You may need a globe for this one!)

Map Skills: West Virginia

Use the map below to answer the questions on page 14.

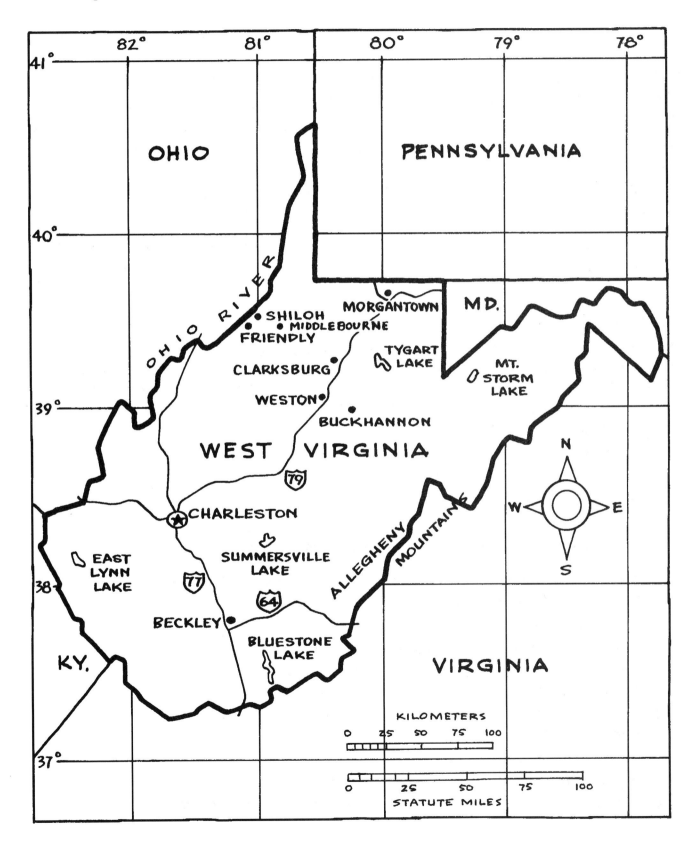

Reading Response Journal

One great way to ensure that the reading of Shiloh becomes a personal experience for each student is to include the use of **Reading Response Journals** in your plans. In these journals, students are encouraged to respond to the story in a number of ways.

- Tell students that the purpose of the journal is to record their thoughts, ideas, observations, and questions as they read *Shiloh.*
- Provide students with stimulating topics from the story or have them find their own. Here are some examples from Section 1:

    —The Prestons live in a rural part of West Virginia, far from the stimulation of cities. How does their lifestyle compare to your own?

    —Marty is outraged by the way Judd Travers treats Shiloh. Marty's father, however, tells his son to mind his own business: "'If it's Travers' dog, it's no mind of ours how he treats it.'" Do you agree with Mr. Preston? How does his argument make you feel?

- After completing each chapter, students can write about what they learned.
- Ask students to draw responses to events in the story.
- Students may enter "diary-like" responses in their journals.
- Encourage students to bring their journal ideas to life through plays, debates, stories, songs, poems, and art displays.
- Have each student respond to quotes from the novel. Afterwards, share the different responses.

Teacher Note: Give students time to write in their journals daily. Explain that their journals can be evaluated in a number of ways.

Personal reflections may be read by the teacher, but no corrections or letter grades will be assigned. Credit is given for effort; anyone who really tries will gain credit. If a grade is desired for a personal entry, grade according to quantity and quality of journal entries. For example, if a student conscientiously completes five out of five journal assignments, he or she receives an "A."

As you read student journals, be sure to respond often and without judgment. Let the student know that you appreciate and enjoy his or her work. Here are a few examples of constructive responses:

    —"You have really discovered what's important in the story."

    —"You write so clearly. It's as if I'm there with you!"

    —"If you feel comfortable, I'd like to share this with the class. I think they'll enjoy it as much as I have."

Quiz Time!

1. On the back of this paper, write a one-paragraph summary of the major events in each chapter of Section 2. Then complete the rest of the questions.

2. Although the Prestons are not "rock poor," they do not have money to save. Where does the Prestons' spare money go?

   _____

   _____

3. As Chapter 5 begins, Marty lists three problems: (1) where to hide Shiloh, (2) keeping Shiloh quiet, (3) how to get food to Shiloh. How are these problems solved?

   _____

   _____

4. What promise does Marty make to Shiloh?

   _____

   _____

5. Marty vividly remembers stealing from Dara Lynn. What does he remember? How did he feel about it? Why is it meaningful to him now?

   _____

   _____

6. How does Marty keep Dara Lynn off the hill where he is hiding Shiloh?

   _____

   _____

7. What do we learn about Judd Travers' childhood? How does Marty respond to Judd's story? Be specific in your answer!

   _____

   _____

8. Describe David Howard's house. How does it compare to Marty's?

   _____

   _____

9. What does Marty purchase at Mr. Wallace's corner store? Why?

   _____

   _____

10. Although he feels badly about it, Marty must lie in order to keep Shiloh safe. List at least three different lies Marty tells in Chapters 4–7.

   _____

   _____

Building a Pen

When Marty decides to keep Shiloh, his first step is to build an animal shelter. Using fencing, wire, and rotten planks, Marty constructs a pen for Shiloh. Here is his description:

"I string the fencing around the trunks of three small trees, for corner posts, and then back to the pine tree again where I fasten it with wire. Pen measures about six by eight feet.

I go back down to the shed again, and this time I get the old rotten planks Dad took out of the back steps when he put in the new. I take the planks up to Shiloh's pen and make him a lean-to at one end, to protect him from rain. Fill the pie tin with water so's he'll have something to drink."

As you can tell, Marty is both knowledgeable and resourceful!

Now, imagine that a group of you find an abused animal that you need to protect. Like Marty, you will need to build a shelter that will provide safety and comfort. Moreover, like Marty, you are not able to buy anything. Everything you use should be from your own households!

Keep the following things in mind as you build a cozy animal shelter.
- Build a lean-to, or a sloped roof, to keep out the rain.
- Be sure to have an entrance that can be tightly shut.
- If you do not have trees nearby, use posts or table legs to anchor the fencing.
- Your shelter should measure six feet by eight feet.
- Provide a drinking dish.
- Be sure to have your parents' permission before using any material!

When you complete your shelter, take a photo of it to share with classmates.

Have fun!

Improvisation!

One great way to experience literature is by acting it out. Sometimes, a great book is adapted into a play or even a movie. (You can probably think of several examples.) Fortunately, you do not need a script in order to perform scenes from *Shiloh*. Instead, you can have fun and sharpen your theatrical skills through improvisation, or theater games. In improvisation, your performance is spontaneous; you make it up as you go along! Before you begin, keep these things in mind:

- Scenes must be from *Shiloh* or contain characters from the book.
- If you are not participating in an improvisation, you are part of the audience.
- There is to be no booing.
- Speak loudly and face the audience.

Remember, you are trying to embrace the spirit of the characters in *Shiloh*. So, try to be genuine in your acting. After each scene, take time for constructive criticism. You may want to question whether or not a character would have behaved a certain way in a scene. Was the incident or conversation believable?

Here is a list of theater games to choose from. You may know some of your own.

Theater Games

1. **Freeze Improvisation**—This is a silent exercise. Two people act out a scene that contains movement. After a minute or so, someone yells "Freeze!" and the two players are motionless. The newcomer steps in, taps one of the actors on the shoulder (the one who has participated longest) and, continuing the same motion, changes the scene.

2. **Audience's Choice**—An audience member chooses two characters from the book. Another person suggests a situation for the characters. For example, someone might suggest "Judd Travers and David Howard go on a camping trip." The players act out the scene!

3. **Radio Interview**—One person acts as a radio announcer, another as a character from a book. This can also take the form of a T.V. talk show panel.

4. **A Scene from the Book**—Simply act out a scene from the book, making up lines as you go along.

5. **Genre Switch!**—First, decide on a scene from the book. Next, choose a director. The scene begins normally, but as it progresses, the director calls out different genres (types of art), and the actors immediately switch genres. Possibilities might include melodrama, Western, opera, gothic, or even science fiction.

Recycling Cans and Bottles

Marty is determined to buy Shiloh from Judd Travers. However, Marty's money-making resources are limited. He really only has one possibility, as his father tells him: "'Collect some bottles, take 'em in for deposit. Pick up some aluminum cans, maybe, for the recycling place.'" Of course, Marty is disheartened. It would take him a long time to raise the money by collecting cans. "Must walk five miles that morning," Marty tells us, "and all I find is seven cans and one bottle." And after long hours of searching, all he has is "fifty-three cents for the cans I collected . . . ."

According to Judd, Shiloh cost $35.00. Suppose Judd were willing to sell Shiloh at that price. In West Virginia, a person is reimbursed approximately 35 cents per pound of aluminum and 30 cents per pound for bottles. How many pounds would Marty need to collect to buy Shiloh? Given Marty's luck so far, how long do you think it would take Marty to make that kind of money?

Now do a little research and find out the recycling rates in your state. Some states have per bottle and per can deposits, while others, like West Virginia, only go by weight. In California, for example, aluminum goes for 85 cents a pound! That's more than double what Marty receives.

After finding the rates for five different states (including your own), fill in the chart below. If you are inclined, start a can drive and buy something for your classroom. Or, in the spirit of *Shiloh,* you can help an animal find a good home!

State	per bottle	per can	per pound aluminum	per pound glass

State	$35.00 will buy how many . . .			
	bottles?	cans?	lbs. aluminum?	lbs. glass?

Word Portrait of an Animal I Love

"Nobody else loves you as much as a dog. Except your ma, maybe."
—Marty Preston

We can all relate to Marty when he falls in love with Shiloh. Most of us have, at one time or another, loved an animal dearly. Use this page to describe an animal you love. Use lots of detailed descriptions of the animal. What is its personality? When and where did you get it? What does it like to do? Attach a photo of your animal in the space provided. Feel free to use the back of this sheet if you need more space.

Quiz Time!

1. On the back of this paper, write a one-paragraph summary of the major events in each chapter of Section 3. Then complete the rest of the questions.

2. Marty feeds Shiloh all kinds of food, even squash. How does Shiloh adjust to this diet?

    _____

    _____

3. "'Folks are taking to leavin' me food in their mailboxes,'" says Mr. Preston. Why does his news make Marty so nervous?

    _____

    _____

4. Why are the townspeople concerned about Mrs. Preston's health? Why are they telling her what to take for headaches?

    _____

    _____

5. After Mrs. Preston discovers Shiloh, Marty comes up with a plan to find his beloved beagle a safe home. What is his plan?

    _____

    _____

6. Briefly describe how Shiloh gets hurt.

    _____

    _____

    _____

7. Describe what takes place at Doc Murphy's house. What are Shiloh's chances of living?

    _____

    _____

8. How does Marty feel after he tells David Howard the truth about Shiloh? How does David respond?

    _____

    _____

    _____

9. Does Dara Lynn support Marty, or does she harass her older brother? Be specific!

    _____

    _____

10. What agreement do the Prestons make with Judd concerning Shiloh?

    _____

    _____

Corn Bread and Cornmeal Mush: Eating Like the Prestons

Although the Prestons cannot afford to eat in luxury, they get by with a healthy diet, a diet that reflects their rural lifestyle and economic status. They rely on simple foods and leftovers, never wasting. Note Mr. Preston's breakfast:

> *". . . he starts in on his breakfast, which is Wheat Chex and any fruit he can get from our peach tree. He makes himself coffee and eats the corn bread or biscuits Ma saves for him from our meal the night before."*

Now compare this to the lunch and dessert Marty receives at David Howard's house:

> "Mrs. Howard made us each a chicken-salad sandwich with lettuce and tomato, and toothpicks with olives on top to hold it all together." To add to that, for dessert Marty devours "tapioca pudding and chocolate-covered graham crackers . . . . " Clearly, these are foods Marty does not have at home.

In order to get a taste of the Prestons' lifestyle, then, we should eat like them. For one day, choose your menu from the list below. Since Marty had a Coke at the gas station, you can have one soda or juice. Otherwise, drink water. Here is a partial list of the foods the Prestons eat at home. You will notice no fast food, pizza, or frozen yogurt!

> *Wheat Chex, Cheerios, oatmeal, toast, bacon, chicken, sausage, biscuits, jam, lard, corn bread, cornmeal mush, peanut-butter-and-soda-cracker sandwich, beans, squash, potato, peaches, meat loaf, rabbit, sour cream, cheese*

After eating like the Prestons for a day, write a paragraph about the experience. Turn this in to your teacher. To help get you started, here is a recipe for corn bread, one of the mainstays of the Prestons' diet:

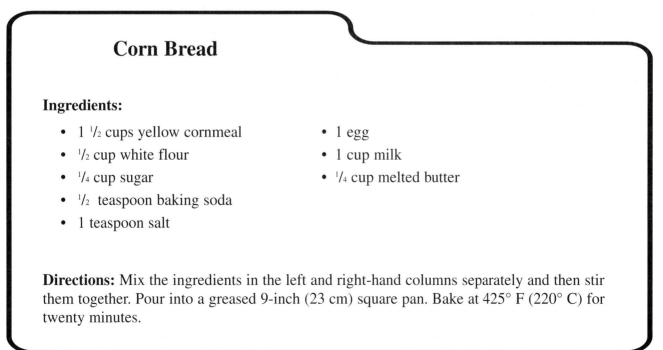

Corn Bread

Ingredients:

- 1 ½ cups yellow cornmeal
- ½ cup white flour
- ¼ cup sugar
- ½ teaspoon baking soda
- 1 teaspoon salt

- 1 egg
- 1 cup milk
- ¼ cup melted butter

Directions: Mix the ingredients in the left and right-hand columns separately and then stir them together. Pour into a greased 9-inch (23 cm) square pan. Bake at 425° F (220° C) for twenty minutes.

Mock Trial: Who Is Shiloh's Rightful Owner?

Imagine Marty were to take Judd Travers to court for the right to own Shiloh. Who do you think would win the case? What would Marty's argument be? What would Judd's argument be? What witnesses would be called upon? What would the judge and jury decide?

Now it is your opportunity to find out. Your class will have a mock trial between Marty and Judd. First, with your teacher's help, choose students to play the following characters in your courtroom drama:

Marty Preston _____ Marty's lawyer _____ Judd Travers _____ Judd's lawyer _____ Judge _____ Witnesses _____ _____ _____ _____ _____	Jury (12 people) _____ _____ _____ _____ _____ _____ _____ _____ _____ _____ _____ _____

The next step is for both sides to gather evidence. Using accounts from the book and real documents, try to gather as many facts as possible. Both sides should try to use the laws about animal ownership to strengthen their argument. Remember, speculation and emotion do not go far in a courtroom! Although most readers probably feel Shiloh belongs to Marty, an objective jury may not. Finally, both sides should study the opposition's argument and be ready to counter it.

There should be an equal number of witnesses for both sides. If someone claims to have seen Judd beating his dogs, for example, then someone else should vouch for the dogs' well-being. Lawyers for both sides should prompt witnesses on what questions to expect. When the day of the trial arrives, participants wear appropriate costumes and play out the trial in character. Do you think Judd would dress up nicely for a day in court? What about Marty? David Howard?

The jury has a very important responsibility. They must listen to the facts and go by the letter of the law as they understand it, even if they think it is unfair.

Finally, consider videotaping the proceedings and showing the tape to parents during an open house.

Point of View

Who should write the story? That is the important decision Phyllis had to make when she sat down to write *Shiloh*. Certainly, the story would be very different if someone other than Marty told it. Imagine if Judd Travers told it! What if it was told by the author herself, someone outside of the story?

It follows that an active reader should always be attentive to the point of view in which a story is told. Then, when you sit down to write your own stories, you will be able to make a knowledgeable choice for point of view.

There are two basic points of view: **first person** and **third person**. If a story is told in first person, then the narrator participates in the story. You can tell a story is in first person when the narrator uses the pronoun **I** to tell the story. Here is an example of first person point of view from *Shiloh*:

> *"I can hear Judd's footsteps coming around the side of the Jeep, and I can smell his chewing tobacco, strong as coffee."*

A third person narrator, on the other hand, stands back and tells a story without participating in it. You can tell a story is in the third person when the narrator uses the pronouns **he, she, it,** and **they** to tell the story. Here is the same sentence as above told in third person:

> *"Marty could hear Judd's footsteps coming around the side of the Jeep, and he could smell his chewing tobacco, strong as coffee."*

Second person is a point of view rarely used in narrative. It refers to the person being addressed. You can tell the story is in second person when the narrator uses the pronouns **you** to tell the story. Here is an example, again using the same sentence:

> *"You could hear Judd's footsteps coming around the side of the Jeep, and you could smell his chewing tobacco, strong as coffee."*

Discuss the different versions with your classmates. Do they affect you differently? Do you agree with Naylor's choice of first person for *Shiloh*? Why or why not?

Practice on a separate sheet of paper by rewriting an episode from Shiloh, using third person point of view. Next, write the same episode from the point of view of a character other than Marty! Afterwards, take turns reading your pieces to the class.

Studying the Beagle

What do we learn about beagles from reading *Shiloh*? Does the story make you want to have a beagle for a pet? Do beagles make good hunting dogs? Are they sensitive? Are they finicky eaters? What do they look like?

Our first step in our study of the beagle is to make a list of everything you learned about Shiloh. After completing the list, use appropriate resource books to research the following questions about the beagle. (Feel free to add your own findings). Give the project to your teacher when you finish. As you will see, Shiloh comes from an ancient, dignified breed of dog.

- What is the origin of the beagle? Is it a young or an old breed?

- When did the beagle first make it to the United States?

- Describe the physical features of the beagle.

- What is the hunting style of the beagle? What do hunters prefer to use them for? Do beagles hunt in packs or alone?

- Some people use beagles as show dogs. What is the size limit for a show beagle?

- What is the best way to care for a beagle, both physically and emotionally?

- Are there organizations for beagle owners? Name them.

- What are the different color variations of the beagle?

- What is the general temperament of the beagle? Do they make good pets? Do they get along well with other dogs?

- Add three more interesting facts about the beagle.

Rural Life and Urban Life

Shiloh is set in West Virginia, which is primarily a rural state. **Rural** refers to country life as opposed to city life. Certainly, Marty lives in a very rural setting. You may remember him saying that there are no street lights where he lives and that "Night in West Virginia is as dark as black can be." **Urban** is the exact opposite; it refers to city life. People who live in Los Angeles, Toronto, or New York City live in urban areas.

The most obvious differences between rural and urban life are, of course, physical ones. Rural dwellers usually enjoy a more natural landscape, free of the hustle and bustle of city life. Urban residents, on the other hand, usually live in more populated areas while enjoying a variety of entertainment and opportunities.

Now we have a chance to look more deeply into the differences between rural and urban living. Compare each of the lifestyles by filling in the chart below. For the rural and urban areas, choose the big city and rural town you are most familiar with. Before beginning, be sure to define the features in the left-hand column. Finally, share your findings with your classmates. Can you come to any conclusions about the characteristics of each lifestyle? Where would you rather live? Why?

	RURAL	URBAN	MY TOWN
Population & Ethnic Diversity			
Natural Life: **Lakes, Forests, Rivers, Etc.**			
Entertainment: **Movies, Concerts, Fairs, Museums, Theaters**			
Quality of Life			

What Would You Do?

From the moment Marty meets Shiloh, he is forced to make difficult decisions, especially for an eleven-year-old boy. Although he knows he is probably breaking the law, he trusts his heart and hides Shiloh, complicating his and his family's life.

Have you ever had to deal with a similar situation? If the answer is yes, then you know the complexity of Marty's dilemma. If the answer is no, then here is your chance to speculate about what you would do. For each of the following situations, write how you would respond. Try to be as realistic and honest as possible. Keep in mind all the consequences of your choices, long term and short term. How much would you be willing to risk? After completing the assignment, get in groups of three or four and share your responses.

1. You find a dog. You know its owner is abusing it, but you cannot prove it. What do you do?

_____

_____

2. You find one hundred dollars on your school grounds. Do you keep it or turn it in to your teacher?

_____

3. The night before the most important test of the year, someone offers you a copy of the answers. What do you do?

_____

4. Your parents have an empty house for rent. One day, you sneak in and find a homeless mother and her three children living there. What do you do?

_____

_____

5. There is an ancient grove of trees in your neighborhood, the only one of its kind in the region. You stand to make lots of money if you cut it down and build condominiums. What do you do?

_____

_____

6. A friend is suffering from a very painful, deadly disease, with no chance of survival. He or she asks you to give him/her a pill that will end his/her life. If you do it, no one will ever find out. What do you do?

_____

_____

Quiz Time!

1. On the back of this paper, write a one-paragraph summary of the major events in each chapter of Section 4. Then complete the rest of the questions.

2. Briefly describe how the Prestons treat Shiloh during his recovery. Are Marty's parents loving towards Shiloh? Do they hold back? What about Dara Lynn and Becky?

   _____

   _____

3. All along, Marty is certain Judd mistreats his animals. Why not, then, just report Judd to the proper authorities?

   _____

   _____

4. According to Marty, what is the fine for killing a doe out of season?

   _____

   _____

5. In order to have Shiloh, Marty agrees to keep silent about the deer. Is he comfortable with this agreement? Explain.

   _____

   _____

6. Judd works Marty very hard. List three of Marty's chores. Are they all necessary?

   _____

   _____

7. What word does Judd leave out of the contract? Why does Marty insist he include it?

   _____

   _____

8. According to Judd, the contract between him and Marty is no good. Why not?

   _____

   _____

9. For a brief moment, Marty feels "a fraction of an ounce sorry" for Judd. What brings on this sudden sympathy?

   _____

   _____

10. After Marty completes his side of the bargain, Judd presents him with a gift. What does he give him? Why is it a significant gesture?

   _____

   _____

Storytelling

"When I was growing up," writes Phyllis Reynolds Naylor, "my mother, and sometimes my father, read aloud to us every night. They sang to us, too, and many of their songs were really stories." This early exposure to storytelling inspired her to become a prolific writer. In fact, she complains that she has so many stories in her head, focusing on one at a time is a challenge!

Everybody has a story to tell. It may be a story about family, friends, or adventure. When you hear someone's personal story, you are participating in oral history. Usually, this history is not written down but passed from one generation to another through storytelling. In every family, there are lots of stories waiting to be discovered.

The first step in discovering these treasures is simply to listen. Ask older friends or relatives to tell you their personal stories. If possible, tape the stories. It is best to prepare some questions to keep the conversation going. Here are a few suggestions. Feel free to add your own questions.

- Do you have a large family? How did you get along with your brothers and sisters?
- What rules did you have around the house when you were young? Do you think the rules were fair? What kinds of things were off limits?
- Describe a meal and/or holiday when you were a child. Perhaps there is a special recipe or tradition you could share.
- What was school like for you? What subjects did you study? What books do you remember reading?
- What games did you enjoy most when you were my age?
- Describe a special event that stands out in your mind.
- Tell a humorous story from your past.
- Were there any hardships you or your parents had to face? How did you overcome them?
- Can you relate any stories your parents passed on to you about their lives?
- What was the greatest challenge to our country when you were growing up? How did it affect your life?
- Describe the most frightening event of your childhood.
- Does today's generation differ from yours in any particular ways? Tell a story or anecdote from your life to illustrate the difference(s).

Become a Storyteller

Pick a few of your favorite stories and practice telling them without notes. Have a storytelling hour in class. Be creative! You might want to try pantomime, use costumes, or play more than one character.

For the teacher: Contact your local library and find out about inviting a storyteller to the class. This will inspire the students while teaching them the art of storytelling.

A Closer Look: Marty and Judd

Most stories contain a *protagonist* and an *antagonist.* The protagonist is the hero, or main character, while the antagonist is often the "bad guy." In *Shiloh,* Marty is the protagonist while Judd is the antagonist. We sympathize with Marty and dislike Judd.

Usually, the antagonist remains hateful. When he or she is defeated, we feel satisfied and righteous. Is this the case in *Shiloh?* At the end of the novel, are we so quick to despise Judd? Certainly, when Marty finally gets Shiloh, he feels differently towards his "enemy."

In groups of three or four, discuss the following questions. Designate one person from the group to write down your responses. Afterwards, share your thoughts with the class. Be sure to use details to support your answers!

- Describe Judd's living environment. Do we ever hear of any friends or family? Do you think he is happy with his life? Is he lonely?

- How do Marty's parents treat Judd? Do you think most of the people in Tyler County approach him the same way? Why?

- In Chapter 6, on his way to David Howard's house, Marty accepts a ride from Judd. What do they talk about? What does Marty learn about Judd? What is the tone of the conversation? Were you surprised by any of it?

- After learning that Shiloh is wounded, Judd arrives at the Prestons. "I'd rather swim in a river full of crocodiles," says Marty, "than face Judd Travers." But somehow, Marty finds the inner strength to be direct with Judd. Where does this strength come from? Give another example of Marty's courage.

- At the end of his forty hours of working for Judd, Marty says, "I don't know how we done it, but somehow we learned to get along." Indeed, their relationship is changed after their time together. How does this transformation happen? Answer the following questions and then write a statement in the space below, explaining how Marty and Judd learn to get along.

When does Judd first do something nice for Marty?

_____

_____

Why does Marty keep his side of the bargain when he knows he might never get to keep Shiloh?

_____

_____

Why does Judd allow Marty to keep Shiloh?

_____

_____

What does Judd learn from Marty? What does Marty learn from Judd?

_____

_____

Dialect and Nonstandard English

"The day Shiloh come, we're having us a big Sunday dinner," says Marty Preston in the opening sentence of *Shiloh*. What if you were to relate the same information? Would you use the same language? Maybe you would say, "The day that Shiloh came, we were having a big Sunday dinner," or "The day Shiloh come first wuz dinnertime Sunday." Of course, all these examples share the same meaning. However, each reflects a different **dialect**, or manner of speaking, that characterizes a certain people or geographical region.

We learn our dialect from the people we grow up with. We hear their language and adopt it as our own. Dialects may differ in vocabulary, pronunciation, and syntax (the way words are put together to form sentences). In most countries, there is a standard dialect. In the United States, this is called standard English; it is the dialect used by news broadcasters, for example. Most of us, however, speak our own dialect. Some writers, such as Mark Twain, Zora Neal Hurston, and, in the case of *Shiloh*, Phyllis Reynolds Naylor, use dialect in their writing. Some novels are narrated in dialect, while others use dialect only in dialogue.

Here are some examples of the rural West Virginian dialect used in *Shiloh*. In groups of two or three, read each of the expressions and determine how it might be said in standard English. Also, try to translate the phrases into another regional dialect.

Example: "Where'd it pick up with you?" means "Where did it start following you?"

1. *Can't keep that coon dog home to save my soul.* _____
   _____

2. *Route takes him 'bout eighty-five miles on roads you could hardly git by on in winter.* _____
   _____

3. *Ma knows me better'n I know myself sometimes, but she don't have this straight.* _____
   _____

4. *I don't pay her no mind at all.* _____
   _____

5. *Hope the others'll learn him something.* _____
   _____

6. *Thinking don't cost nothing.* _____
   _____

Pick out four more examples of dialect from *Shiloh*. Write them down and translate them into standard English. Next, in a small group, brainstorm to uncover some examples of your own dialect. What kinds of phrases are common to your community or family? _____

_____

_____

_____

_____

Lying and Personal Ethics

> *"A lie. That's a flat-out lie. Funny how one lie leads to another and before you know it, your whole life can be a lie."*
>
> *"A lie don't seem like a lie anymore when it's meant to save a dog, and right and wrong's all messed up in my head."*
>
> —Marty Preston

As you can tell from the quotes above, Marty Preston is wrestling with his personal ethics, or moral principles. Although the sin of lying is pretty clear to him most of the time, he is in a situation which turns his ethics upside down. When he lied about stealing chocolate from Dara Lynn, for example, he felt guilty and knew he did wrong. But when it comes to protecting Shiloh, Marty does not know the right path to take. Finally, he prays: "Jesus . . . which do you want me to do? Be one hundred percent honest and carry that dog back to Judd so that one of your creatures can be kicked and starved...or keep him here and fatten him up to glorify your creation?" Marty chooses to protect Shiloh.

But choosing Shiloh is complicated. Not only is Marty lying to Judd but also to his family and friends. Soon, he is lying to the entire town of Friendly! Before he knows it, his lies have caused all sorts of misunderstandings.

Now we will take a closer look at the question of lying, both in *Shiloh* and in your own life. Complete the assignments below and then go to the next page.

Write at least one lie Marty tells to each of the following people:

- his mom   _____
  _____
- his dad   _____
  _____
- Dara Lynn   _____
  _____
- Judd Travers   _____
  _____
- David Howard   _____
  _____
- Mrs. Howard   _____
  _____
- Mr. Wallace.   _____
  _____

Circle every lie you think Marty had to tell in order to keep Shiloh safe.

Give at least two examples of how the lies grow. How do Marty's lies affect his family? (Be specific!)

Lying and Personal Ethics *(cont.)*

Reflection

Respond to the following questions, using separate paper if needed. Be sure to give specific examples. Feel free to discuss these questions with classmates or family members.

1. Marty is encouraged by his family and his religion to tell the truth. Where do you get your ethical standards? Can you recall a specific incident when you were talked to about lying?

   _____

2. When Marty tells Judd Travers that he had not seen Shiloh in the yard, he was lying by omission, or telling a "white lie." In your opinion, is lying by omission less severe than telling an outright lie? Why?

   _____

3. Is it ever okay to lie? If so, give examples of situations when lying is acceptable. If not, explain why "honesty is the best policy."

   _____

4. Although Marty is concerned about lying to his family, ultimately he feels he has to answer to God. Suddenly, he is questioning what he has been taught all his life. He would rather go to hell, for instance, than stay in heaven without Shiloh. Is it right for Marty to question what he has been told by his elders? Have you ever been in a situation which compelled you to do the same?

   _____

5. Marty's dad seems to know Judd mistreats his dogs, but he feels nothing can be done about it. Is Marty's dad being dishonest?

   _____

6. Marty's final lie is his most difficult. Should he have kept silent about Judd shooting the doe? Was this lie more acceptable than the others? Why?

   _____

7. Marty is very aware of the lies he tells, reporting them honestly. Now, describe a lie you told sometime in your life. Why did you lie? How did you feel afterwards? Have you ever felt, like Marty, that you had to lie for a good cause? Explain.

   _____

8. When Marty's dad learns that his son and wife are keeping secrets from him, he is very upset. Describe a time you were lied to. Why did the person(s) lie? How did you feel afterwards?

   _____

9. Have you ever lied to yourself? Explain.

   _____

Any Questions?

When you finished reading *Shiloh,* did you have any questions that were left unanswered?
Write some of your questions here.

_____

_____

_____

Now write possible answers to some of the unanswered questions, both your own and the
ones below. Feel free to work in groups or by yourself.

- Is Judd Travers going to try to get Shiloh back?

- Does Marty ever tell anyone about Judd killing the doe out of season?

- Do Shiloh's wounds heal up completely, or is he left with a limp?

- Do Marty and Judd become friends?

- Is Judd kinder to his dogs now?

- Does Mrs. Preston ever find out why people thought she was not well?

- Does Mr. Preston ever discover why people were leaving him extra food?

- Will Shiloh be Mr. Preston's hunting companion? How would Marty feel?

- Are the Prestons going to see better times financially? Will feeding Shiloh be a
  financial burden?

- Does Mr. Wallace find out why Marty spent fifty-three cents on cheap food?

- Will Marty pay Doc Murphy for Shiloh's vet bills?

- Will Mr. Baker's German shepherd threaten Shiloh again?

- Is Marty at peace with himself after all the falsehoods he told?

- How does Mr. Preston feel about Marty's actions? Does he still feel Marty acted
  wrongly in regard to Shiloh and Judd?

- Does Marty find any way to earn money besides can and bottle collecting?

Descriptive Writing

In the story *Shiloh*, the author uses descriptive writing to give the reader a sharply focused picture of the rural West Virginia where Marty Preston lives. Read the descriptions below, taken from Marty's world. In the space provided, write your own descriptions of your world compared to Marty's world. Use precise words and colorful language.

Marty's World	Your World
(page 12) "You ask me the best place to live, I'd say right where we are, a little four-room house with hills on three sides."	"You ask me the best place to live, I'd say _____ _____ _____
(page 13) "My favorite place to walk is just across this rattly bridge where the road curves by the old Shiloh school house and follows the river. River to one side, trees the other — sometimes a house or two."	"My favorite place to walk is _____ _____ _____
(page 21) "I want to be a vet someday . . . . I want to be a traveling vet. The kind that has his office in a van and goes around to people's homes, don't make folks come to him."	"I want to be a _____ someday. _____ _____ _____
(page 22) "Dusk is settling in now. Still warm though. A warm July night. Trees look dark against the red sky; lights coming on in a house here, another one there."	""Dusk is settling in now. _____ _____ _____
(page 29) "Can you think of a way I can earn some money?" "Collect some bottles...pick up some aluminum cans for the recycling place."	"Can you think of a way to earn some money? _____ _____ _____
(page 44) "I'm tense as a cricket that night."	"I'm tense as _____ _____ _____ _____
(page 55) "Night in West Virginia is as dark as black can be. No car lights sweepin' across my walls . . . no street lights shining in the windows."	"Night in _____ is _____ _____ _____"
(page 121) "Way we're raised around, children don't talk back to grown folks. Don't hardly talk much at all, in fact. Learn to listen, keep your mouth shut . . . ."	" _____ _____ _____"

Book Report Ideas

There are many ways to report on a book. After completing *Shiloh*, choose a method of reporting on the book. Pick from the list below or decide on one of your own ideas.

• A Visual Report

Create a visual report through sculpture, drawing, collage, or mural. Some popular methods include drawing a life-sized representation of a main character, crafting a scene inside a shoe box, or making a "board game" of the book.

• Time Capsule

Imagine people in the future coming across *Shiloh*. Inside a time capsule design, convince these people why they should read *Shiloh*.

• Come to Life!

A group acts out a scene from the book, attending to costumes, props, and dialogue. Afterwards, they relate the significance of the scene to the entire book.

• Add a Chapter

Add a chapter to *Shiloh*. The chapter can take place within the story line or afterwards. Try to emulate Phyllis Reynolds Naylor's writing style.

• A Character Comes to Life!

Suppose one of the characters from *Shiloh* walked into your classroom! There are two ways to approach this report: (1) write about what the character sees, hears, and feels as he or she experiences your world and (2) perform the character by dressing up in costume and delivering a speech from the character's point of view.

• Dust Jacket Design

Design a dust jacket for the novel. Include the title, author, and an important scene, image, or character on the cover. Include a book summary on the inside flaps, and on the back a *teaser*—an appealing hint about the book like "This heartwarming novel could win new fans."

• Book Review

Write a book review about *Shiloh*. Use real book reviews for your models.

• Multimedia Presentation

Illustrate the story through a multimedia presentation. Consider using music, video, slides, narration, and film strips.

Research Activity: The Newbery Medal

Since 1921, the John Newbery Medal has been awarded annually. This prestigious award is given to the "most distinguished contribution to American literature for children." *Shiloh* won the award in 1992.

Here is a list of the Newbery winners from 1922 - 1946, along with the author's last name and the publisher. You might not be familiar with some of these titles. Read one of the books from the list. Afterwards, give a five-to-ten-minute oral presentation to your class about the book.

1922 *The Story of Mankind*
Van Loon (Liveright)

1923 *The Voyages of Dr. Doolittle*
Lofting (Lippincott)

1924 *The Dark Frigate*
Hawes (Little, Brown)

1925 *Tales from Silver Lands*
Finger (Doubleday)

1926 *Shen of the Sea*
Chrisman (Duttong)

1927 *Smoky, the Cowhorse*
James (Scribner)

1928 *Gay-Neck*
Mukerji (Dutton)

1929 *The Trumpeter of Krakow*
Kelly (Macmillan)

1930 *Hitty, Her First Hundred Years*
Field (Macmillan)

1931 *The Cat Who Went to Heaven*
Coatsworth (Macmillan)

1932 *Waterless Mountain*
Armer (McKay)

1933 *Young Fu of the Upper Yangtze*
Lewis (Holt)

1934 *Invincible Louisa*
Meigs (Little, Brown)

1935 *Dorby*
Shannon (Viking)

1937 *Roller Skates*
Sawyer (Viking)

1938 *The White Stag*
Seredy (Viking)

1939 *Thimble Summer*
Enright (Holt)

1940 *Daniel Boone*
Daughtery (Viking)

1941 *Call It Courage*
Sperry (Macmillan)

1942 *The Matchlock Gun*
Edmonds (Dodd, Mead)

1943 *Adam of the Road*
Gray (Viking)

1944 *Johnny Tremain*
Forbes (Houghton Mifflin)

1945 *Rabbit Hill*
Lawson (Viking)

1946 *Strawberry Girl*
Lenski (Lippincott)

Add a Chapter, *Shiloh* Style!

Have you ever wondered what it takes to write a short story or a novel? Did Phyllis Reynolds Naylor, for example, figure out the entire plot of *Shiloh* before she began the novel? Or were there surprises along the way? Did she develop the characters in depth, or did the characters develop as the story matured? How much rewriting took place? How long did it take her to write *Shiloh?* Did she work on a computer? Did she research Tyler County? Did she keep notes on the rural dialect?

Certainly, each writer works differently, but they all must attend to some of the same basic problems, including plot, tone, and point of view. Now it is your chance to taste the writing process. Working alone or in small groups, add a chapter to *Shiloh.* Begin by reading the following quote very carefully:

> *"I'm wondering how things would have turned out if it hadn't been for that deer. If I'd just knocked on Judd's front door two weeks ago and told him I wasn't giving Shiloh up, what would have happened then?"*
>
> —Marty Preston

Your job is to answer Marty's question: "What would have happened then?" Here are a few rules to follow as you write your chapter:

- You are writing the chapter as if it were to be included in the book. In other words, you are imitating the tone and style of *Shiloh.* (Before beginning, study the next page for more specifics on writing style and tone.)

- Use appropriate West Virginian dialect. You will need to review some of Marty's and Judd's phrases before beginning.

- The chapter can begin with Marty walking through the woods or knocking at Judd's door.

- The chapter should have some kind of ending, although the situation itself does not need to be resolved. For example, Marty may run off, frightened, with Judd threatening to hurt Shiloh.

- The chapter should be a minimum of two pages. The final product should be presented neatly, either handwritten in ink, typewritten, or word processed.

- Remember to strive for believability. It is doubtful, for instance, that Judd and Marty would become best friends and have a picnic in the woods. It is also doubtful that Judd would shoot Marty.

- Be prepared to read your completed chapter to the class.

Add a Chapter, *Shiloh* Style! *(cont.)*

Dialect, Grammar, and Vocabulary

One of the characteristics of *Shiloh* is Naylor's use of dialect, or non-standard English. By having Marty, an eleven-year-old boy, write in the way he talks, Naylor makes the book friendly and personal. And with this dialect, she has the freedom to change some of the rules of grammar. Note, for instance, the first sentence of the book: *"The day Shiloh come, we're having us a big Sunday dinner."* Of course, this is not proper grammar; Marty should have used the past tense, came. Why does he use come instead? Because that is the way he speaks.

There are many other examples of sentence variation that come from dialect, including the use of fragments, or incomplete sentences. Here, Marty describes a fight with Dara Lynn: *"Threw a box of Crayolas at me and could have broke my nose."* Although the sentence is missing a subject, it is clear that Marty meant Dara Lynn.

Dialect also brings with it word choice and variation, especially contractions. A short list of these words includes *tellin', doin', 'em, 'cause, 'specially, better'n.* You should also be aware of phrases, like *"easy as pie," "Just for devilment,"* and *"every which way."* Also, be sure not to use elevated vocabulary. Remember, Marty is telling the story.

As you write your chapter, try to include these variations in grammar and vocabulary. However, be careful not to overdo it. After all, most of the verb tenses are correct, most of the sentences are complete, and most of the words are standard. Remember, the writing must always remain clear!

Tone

Establishing and maintaining a tone for a story is vital to its success. But what exactly is tone? Imagine Marty reading the book aloud to you. What would his voice sound like? Would it be in a hurry? Would it be intense? sad? melancholy? slow? spirited? thoughtful? You probably need several words to describe the tone of *Shiloh*. Take a minute to write down some tone words for the story. Now that the tone is established, try to maintain it as you write your chapter.

Chapter Cover Design

After you complete your chapter, you will be designing a cover for it. The cover is representative of the chapter, not the story as a whole. Take some time to consider the cover design. How much do you want to reveal? What would capture the reader's eye?

On the back of the cover, write a brief summary and some fictitious blurbs about the book. Take a look at *Shiloh* to get an idea.

Add a Chapter, *Shiloh* Style! *(cont.)*

Create your own chapter cover using the border below or design your own border. Color and add appropriate details, such as a rural countryside.

Objective Test and Essay

Matching: Match the descriptions of the characters with their names.

1. _____ Marty Preston	a. gentle but frank mother of three
2. _____ Mrs. Preston	b. Marty's friend from Friendly
3. _____ Mr. Preston	c. grocery story owner
4. _____ Judd Travers	d. a teacher, likes to talk about politics
5. _____ Mr. Wallace	e. 11-year-old boy in love with a beagle
6. _____ Doc Murphy	f. 7 years old, curious but afraid of snakes
7. _____ David Howard	g. Shiloh's personal veterinarian
8. _____ Mrs. Howard	h. chews tobacco, had a tough childhood
9. _____ Dara Lynn	i. youngest of the Prestons
10. _____ Becky	j. postman, hardworking father of three

True or False: Answer true or false in the blanks below.

1. _____ The Prestons live in North Carolina.

2. _____ Shiloh is a hunting dog.

3. _____ Judd and Marty's relationship ends on a sour note.

4. _____ David Howard has a pet hermit crab.

5. _____ The Prestons have street lights near their home.

Sequence: Put these events in order by number 1 to 5 on the lines.

_____ Marty's mom catches Marty and Shiloh.

_____ Judd gives Marty a dog collar.

_____ Marty builds the pen for Shiloh.

_____ Mr. Baker's German shepherd attacks Shiloh.

_____ Marty goes on the postal route with his dad.

Short Answer: In the spaces below, write a brief response to each question.

1. Name a few of the towns in Tyler County. _____

_____

2. What will Marty do if Shiloh is not allowed in heaven? _____

_____

3. What call does Shiloh respond to when Marty finds him? _____

_____

Essay: Respond to the following essay question on the back of this paper. By the end of *Shiloh*, Marty Preston is totally committed to keeping Shiloh. He is even willing to risk his life. Discuss the importance of commitment in determining the outcome of the story. What if Marty had not been committed?

Essay Challenge: Include in your essay the definition of commitment.

Response

Explain the meaning of each of these quotations from Shiloh.

Chapter 1   "And then I feel my heart squeeze up the way he stops smiling, sticks his tail between his legs again, and slinks off."

Chapter 2   "My dream sort of leaks out like water in a paper bag."

Chapter 4   "Ma knows me better'n I know myself sometimes, but she don't have this straight. I don't want just any dog. I want Shiloh, because he needs me. Needs me bad."

Chapter 4   "Strangest thing I ever see in a dog, to be that still."

Chapter 6   "'And right this very minute Jesus is looking down with the saddest eyes on the person who ate that chocolate.'"

Chapter 6   "I like David Howard fine, but I sure don't want him up here."

Chapter 6   "'Sorry's something I can do without.'"

Chapter 7   "First time I ever saw any envy in my ma."

Chapter 7   "I don't feel good about the lies I tell Dara Lynn or David or his ma. But don't feel exactly bad, neither.

Chapter 9   "You aren't fixing to run off with this dog, are you? Marty, don't you ever run away from a problem."

Chapter 9   "And I'm bent over there in the beam of Dad's flashlight, bawling, and I don't even care."

Chapter 10   "But it's my story to tell, not Dad's, and he always did make us face up to what we'd done."

Chapter 10   (Mr. Preston) "'I want you to do what's right.' (Marty) 'What's right?' For once in my eleven years, I think I have my dad stumped.'"

Chapter 13   "Halfway through the woods I'm thinking that what I'm about to do could get my dad in a whole lot of trouble."

Chapter 14   "Been scared most my life of Judd Travers, and here I am, half his size, talking like a grown person."

Chapter 14   "I begin to see now I'm not better than Judd Travers, willing to look the other way to get something I want."

Chapter 15   "I look at the dark closing in, sky getting more and more purple, and I'm thinking how nothing is as simple as you guess—not right or wrong, not Judd Travers, not even me or this dog I got here."

Conversations

Work in size-appropriate groups to write or perform the conversations that might have occurred in each of the following situations.

- Mr. Preston delivers Judd's mail to his front door. (2 people)

- Mrs. Preston and Mrs. Howard have lunch together. (2 people)

- Dara Lynn and Marty go hiking on the hill near their house. Dara Lynn is frightened of the snakes. (2 people)

- At dinner, the Preston's discuss how they will keep Shiloh fed. (5 people)

- Marty is out running with Shiloh. They meet Judd, shotgun in hand. (2 people)

- Marty and Mr. Preston visit Mr. Baker to discuss the danger of his German shepherd getting loose again. (3 people)

- Marty and his parents talk about lying. (3 people)

- Marty and Doc Murphy talk about payment for Shiloh's vet bills. (2 people)

- Marty talks to Doc Murphy about his dream to become a veterinarian. (2 people)

- Judd joins the Prestons for dinner. Shiloh is present. (6 people)

- Marty finds Judd shooting another deer out of season. (2 people)

- Judd asks Marty if he can take Shiloh hunting for a day. He promises to treat Shiloh well. (2 people)

- Dara Lynn and Becky fantasize about the kinds of dogs they want. (2 people)

Bibliography of Related Readings

Fiction

Armstrong, William. *Sounder.* (Harper Collins, 1989)

Cleary, Beverly. *Strider.* (Morrow, 1991)

George, Jean Craighead. *My Side of the Mountain.* (Puffin, 1992)

Kjelgaard, Jim. *Big Red.* (Bantam, 1992)
——— . *Snowdog.* (Bantam, 1983)

Knight, Eric M. *Lassie Come Home.* (Dell, 1939)

London, Jack. *The Call of the Wild.* (Macmillan, 1965)
——— . *White Fang.* (Macmillan, 1935)

Mikaelsen, Ben. *Rescue Josh McGuire.* (Hyperion, 1991)

Morey, Walt. *Scrub Dog of Alaska.* (Blue Heron, 1989)

Mowat, Farley. *The Dog Who Wouldn't Be.* (Bantam, 1981)

Naylor, Phyllis Reynolds. *Josie's Troubles.* (Antheneum, 1992)
——— . *Night Cry.* (Antheneum, 1984)
——— . *Send No Blessings.* (Antheneum, 1990)
——— . *Shiloh.* (Dell, 1991)

Paulsen, Gary. *Dogsong.* (Puffin, 1987)
——— . *Woodsong.* (Puffin, 1991)

Rawls, Wilson. *Where the Red Fern Grows.*(Bantam, 1984)

Nonfiction

American Kennel Club. *The Complete Dog Book.* (Howell Book House, 1973)

Hess, Lilo. *A Dog by Your Side.* (Scribner, 1977)

Musladin, Judith M. *The New Beagle.* (Howell Books, 1990)

Shull, Peg. *The Children of Appalachia.*(Messner, 1969)

Dear Students:

I'm so glad you liked my book *SHILOH*. The first part of the story is true—the way Marty Preston found Shiloh along the river. That's the way I came across the skinny, trembling dog who became Shiloh in my story. It followed my husband and me back to the home of friends in the little community of Shiloh, West Virginia, just up the hill from Friendly.

After we left for home that day, I worried about what would happen to the dog. We weren't sure it didn't belong to someone, and because we had two cats back in Maryland, we didn't take the dog with us. But I couldn't get it out of my mind, and so, shortly after I got home, I began writing the book SHILOH, working out for myself what might have happened if I had known to whom the dog belonged, and what I might have done if I had known it was being mistreated. I don't own a dog now, but I grew up with a springer spaniel, and know what it is like to love a dog.

About three weeks after I started the book, I received a call from our friends in West Virginia. They said that they had gone out for a walk, and the same dog followed them home. It was actually a female. This time they fed her, cleaned her up, took her to the vet to help make her strong and healthy, and named her Clover. Now she is the happiest dog in West Virginia. In fact, the shy, skinny dog who became Shiloh in my book is now a celebrity in the community. Our friends get many requests to bring the dog to schools and libraries, where they put Clover up on a table, and the children line up with their copies of the book. The librarian presses one of Clover's paws on a stamp pad, and then "paw-tographs" the children's books. Clover loves all the attention.

Usually I think about a book a year or two before I ever write any words on paper. I make notes and summaries, so that by the time I start the actual writing, I have a thick notebook full of ideas. Then I write two drafts in longhand before I put the words on a word processor. I change and edit and revise until I can't think of one paragraph, one sentence, or even one word that could be made better. The whole writing process takes about four months. But in this case, I was so upset and worried about the dog that I wrote the first draft in eight weeks.

If you enjoy books about animals, you might also like my novel, *The GRAND ESCAPE*, about our two cats; *JOSIE'S TROUBLES; NIGHT CRY*; and *THE FEAR PLACE*, set in the Rocky Mountains. And perhaps you'll be happy to know that there is a sequel to SHILOH coming out in the fall of 1996. It will be called *SHILOH SEASON*. I did not think I would ever write a sequel, but I had to know what happened next. I hope you like it.

Best wishes,

Phyllis Naylor

(used with permission of the author)

Shiloh

Answer Key

Page 11

1. Accept appropriate responses.

2. On one of his late afternoon strolls, Marty spotted the dog by the Shiloh schoolhouse. Shiloh followed shyly along until Marty whistled. That is when Shiloh exploded with affection. He followed Marty all the way home.

3. The three children are Marty, 11; Dara Lynn, 7; and Becky, 3.

4. Mr. Preston is a mail carrier. Marty wants to be a veterinarian.

5. The story takes place in Friendly, West Virginia. It is summertime.

6. Four reasons Marty does not like Judd: 1. caught Judd cheating Mr. Wallace at the cash register 2. spits tobacco 3. he blocked Marty's view at the fairgrounds 4. kills deer out of season.

7. Marty sleeps on the couch because there isn't room anywhere else. He does not complain.

8. Judd kicks Shiloh. Later, he doesn't feed him dinner. Marty is upset by Judd's actions.

9. Judd subscribes to *Guns and Ammo* and *Shooting Times*. Accept appropriate responses.

10. Marty wants to save money by collecting aluminum cans.

Page 15

1. Accept between 75–80 miles and 125–135 kilometers. (Using 1 km= .6 miles)

2. Maryland

3. Kentucky

4. W. Virginia is between about 37–40 degrees latitude. (Accept more precise answers.)

5. W. Virginia is between about 78–83 degrees longitude (Accept more precise answers.)

6. Friendly is at about 39.5° latitude and 81° longitude.

7. Highway 77 crosses north to south. It covers about 225–250 miles (375 km).

8. Summerville Lake, Sutton Lake, Mt. Storm Lake, Tygart Lake, and Bluestone Lake

9. Virginia

10. W. Virginia is in the northern hemisphere.

Page 17

1. Accept appropriate answers

2. The Prestons' spare money goes to Grandma Preston.

3. 1. Marty hides Shiloh in a pen on the hill, 2. Shiloh naturally stays quiet, 3. Marty gets food for Shiloh by saving his dinner and pocketing small scraps.

4. Marty promises Shiloh that Judd Travers will never kick him again.

5. Marty remembers eating the ear off of one of Dara Lynn's chocolate rabbits and lying to his mother. Afterwards, he felt terrible and then confessed. It is meaningful now because he is telling lies and wrestling with his conscience.

6. Marty keeps Dara Lynn off the hill by telling her it is snake infested.

7. We learn that Judd was beaten by his father. Marty feels sorry for him.

8. David Howard's house has two floors and four bedrooms (specific answers may vary). Marty's house is meager in comparison.

9. At Mr. Wallace's store, Marty spends the 53 cents he earns collecting cans. He asks Mr. Wallace for old food so that he may feed Shiloh.

10. Some of the lies Marty tells include, 1. telling Dara Lynn the hill has snakes, 2. telling his dad he is looking for ground hogs on the hill, 3. telling his mom he wants to save food for after dinner, 4. telling Judd he has not seen his dog, 5. telling Mrs. Howard that his mom has had a headache.

Answer Key (con't.)

Page 22

1. Accept appropriate responses.
2. At first, Shiloh has trouble keeping the food down. Soon after, he eats anything.
3. This news makes Marty nervous because he had asked Mr. Wallace for cheap food. Thus, Mr. Wallace thinks the Prestons have fallen on hard times.
4. The townspeople are concerned about Mrs. Preston's health because Marty told Mrs. Howard that his mom was suffering from headaches.
5. Marty plans to save Shiloh by holding up a sign by the side of the road. The sign would say something like "FREE WORLD'S BEST DOG."
6. Shiloh gets hurt when Baker's German shepherd leaps into his pen and attacks.
7. At Doc Murphy's, Shiloh is stitched up. The doctor finds out Shiloh is Judd's dog. Marty and his dad go home, unsure of Shiloh's survival.
8. Marty feels relieved after he tells David Howard about Shiloh. David is mesmerized and has a hard time letting Marty tell the story!
9. Dara Lynn is very supportive. She tells Marty he was right to keep Shiloh because "'Judd Travers don't take care of his dog...'"
10. The Prestons and Judd agree that Shiloh will be returned once his wounds are healed.

Page 29

1. Accept appropriate answers.
2. Marty's parents are reserved but increasingly affectionate towards Shiloh. Marty's sisters are in love with the dog.
3. Marty knows that the authorities will not have time for an animal abuse case. He also knows that he has no proof that Judd is mistreating his dogs.
4. The fine for killing a doe out of season is $200.00.
5. Keeping silent about the doe is not easy for Marty. He feels guilty about lying and about leaving more deer unprotected.
6. Some of Marty's chores include cutting weeds, mowing grass, hoeing corn, picking beans, cutting wood, and digging holes. Accept supported statements.

7. Judd leaves out the name Shiloh. Marty insists Judd include the name in case he tries to give him another dog.
8. Judd says the contract is no good because they had no witness.
9. Marty feels sorry for Judd after he learns that Judd's father took him hunting only once or twice.
10. When Marty completes his work, Judd gives him a dog collar. It is a sign of their camaraderie, their newly found understanding of one another.

Page 42

Matching

1. e 2. a 3. j 4. h 5. c 6. g 7. b 8. d 9. f 10. i

True or False

1. False 2. True 3. False 4. True 5. False

Sequence

3, 5, 2, 4, 1

Short Answer

1. Some towns in Tyler County include Friendly, Parkersburg, and Middlebourne.
2. Marty will not go to heaven if Shiloh is not allowed in.
3. Shiloh responds to a whistle.

Essay

Answers will vary. Accept all reasonable and well-supported responses.

Essay Challenge

Answers are entirely subjective. Accept all reasonable responses. **Note:** This response should be considered "extra" and not a mandatory part of the test.

Page 43

Accept all reasonable and well-supported responses and explanations.

Page 44

Perform the conversations in class. Ask students to respond to the conversations in several different ways, such as, "Are the conversations realistic?" or, "Are the words the characters say in keeping with their personalities?"